MW01295008

Table of Contents

What is a novena?

The word "novena" is derived from the Latin word for nine, or "novem." a novena is a nine day period of private or public prayer to obtain special graces, to implore special favors, or make special petitions. Many novenas begin or end on a Saint's feast day.

There are some exceptions. Some novenas can range from 5 days, 25 days or more. Some can be said in a single day.

My Recommendation

When I pray novenas I like to go all out. I'll spend one to two hours every day praying all my favorite novenas to our Lord and to most of my favorite Saints. I like to really put forth the effort. To make time and show my devotion.

In times of great need I will pray them every day before mass. Then light a candle after.

God bless you. I hope our Lord answers all of your prayers!

CN.

Sacred Heart of Jesus

Feast Day: June 19.

I. O my Jesus, you have said: 'Truly I say to you, ask and you will receive, seek and you will find, knock and it will be opened to you. ' Behold I knock, I seek and ask for the grace of...... (here name your request)

(Our Father... . Hail Mary... . Glory Be to the Father... .)

Sacred Heart of Jesus, I place all my trust in you.

II. O my Jesus, you have said: 'Truly I say to you, if you ask anything of the Father in my name, he will give it to you. ' Behold, in your name, I ask the Father for the grace of...... . (here name your request)

(Our Father... Hail Mary... . Glory Be To the Father... .)

Sacred Heart of Jesus, I place all my trust in you.

III. O my Jesus, you have said: 'Truly I say to you, heaven and earth will pass away but my words will not pass away. ' Encouraged by your infallible words I now ask for the grace of..... . (here name your request)

(Our Father... . Hail Mary... . Glory Be to the Father...)

Sacred Heart of Jesus, I place all my trust in you.

O Sacred Heart of Jesus, for whom it is impossible not to have compassion on the afflicted, have pity on us miserable sinners and grant us the grace which we ask of you, through the Sorrowful and Immaculate Heart of Mary, your tender Mother and ours.

Say the Hail, Holy Queen and add: St. Joseph, foster father of Jesus, pray for us.

-- St. Margaret Mary Alacoque

Padre Pio recited this novena every day for all those who requested his prayers.

Ancient Prayer to St. Joseph

Feast Day: March 19 and May 1.

(Over 1900 years old)

O St. Joseph, whose protection is so great, so strong, so prompt before the Throne of God, I place in you all my interests and desires. O St. Joseph, do assist me by your powerful intercession and obtain for me from your Divine Son all spiritual blessings through Jesus Christ, Our Lord; so that having engaged here below your Heavenly power I may offer my thanksgiving and homage to the most loving of Fathers. O St. Joseph, I never weary contemplating you and Jesus asleep in your arms. I dare not approach while He reposes near your heart. Press him in my name and kiss His fine Head for me, and ask Him to return the Kiss when I draw my dying breath. St. Joseph, Patron of departing souls, pray for us. Amen.

"This prayer was found in the 50th year of our Lord and Savior Jesus Christ. In 1505, it was sent from the pope to Emperor Charles when he was going into battle. Whoever shall read this prayer or hear it or keep it about themselves, shall never die a sudden death or be drowned, nor shall poison take effect on them; neither shall they fall into the hands of the enemy or be burned in any fire or be overpowered in battle.

Say for nine mornings for anything you desire. It has never been known to fail."

St. Anthony of Padua

Feast Day: June 15.

O wonderful St. Anthony, glorious on account of the fame of your miracles, and through the condescension of Jesus in coming in the form of a little child to rest in your arms, obtain for me of His bounty the grace which I ardently desire from the depths of my heart . (State your intention)

You who were so compassionate toward miserable sinners, regard not the unworthiness of those who pray to you, but the glory of God that it may once again be magnified by the granting of the particular request (State your intention) which I now ask for with persevering earnestness. Amen

Pray one Our Father, one Hail Mary, and Glory Be to the Father, in honor of Saint Anthony.

Saint Anthony, pray for us!

St. Therese, The Little Flower

Feast Day: October 1.

5-Day Novena Prayer to St. Therese

"St. Therese, the Little Flower, please pick me a rose from the Heavenly Garden and send it to me with a message of love.

Ask God to grant me the favor I thee implore, (mention petition here out loud or in silence) and tell Him I will love Him each day more and more. Amen. "

Pray the above prayer along with 5 Our Father's, 5 Hail Mary's, and 5 Glory Be.

On the 5th day pray 5 more Our Father's, Hail Mary's and Glory Be.

St. Jude

(Desperate Situations and Hopeless Cases)

Feast Day: October 28.

O Holy St Jude!

Oh holy St. Jude, apostle and martyr, great in virtue and rich in miracles, near Kinsman of Jesus Christ, faithful intercessor of all who invoke your special patronage in time of need. To you I have recourse from the depth of my hear and humbly beg to whom God has given such great power to come to my assistance. Help me in my present urgent petition, in return I promise to make your name known and cause you to be invoked. St. Jude pray for us and all who invoke your aid. Amen.

Say three Our Fathers, three Hail Marys, and three Glory Be To The Father.

Publication must be promised. This novena has never known to fail.

Holy Spirit

Pentecost.

O Holy Spirit, Divine Consoler!

I adore you as my True God.

I bless You by uniting myself to the praises

You receive from the angel and saints.

I offer You my whole heart,

and I render You heartfelt thanks

for all the benefits You have bestowed

and do unceasingly bestow upon the world.

You are the author of all supernatural gifts

and who did enrich with immense favors the soul

of the Blessed Virgin Mary,

the Mother of God,

I beseech you to visit me by Your grace and Your love,

and grant me the favor

I so earnestly seek in this novena...

(State your request here...)

O Holy Spirit,

spirit of truth,

come into our hearts:

shed the brightness of your light on all nations,

that they may be of one faith and pleasing to You.

Amen.

Come, O Holy Spirit,

fill the hearts of your faithful,

and kindle in them the fire of Your love.

Infant Of Prague

Feast Day: January 14.

This novena can be said for 9 consecutive days or 9 consecutive hours.

O Jesus, Who has said,

ask and you shall receive,

seek and you shall find,

knock and it shall be opened to you,

through the intercession of Mary,

Your Most Holy Mother, I knock,

I seek, I ask that my prayer be granted.

(Make your request)

O Jesus, Who has said,

all that you ask of the Father in My Name,

He will grant you through the intercession of Mary.

Your Most Holy Mother.

I humbly and urgently ask Your Father

in Your Name that my prayer be granted.

(Make your request)

O Jesus, Who has said,

"Heaven and earth shall pass away

but My word shall not pass",

through the intercession of Mary,

Your Most Holy Mother,

I feel confident that my prayer will be granted.

(Make your request)

Mother Of Perpetual Help

Feast Day: June 27.

Mother of Perpetual Help, behold at your feet a sinner who has recourse to you and has confidence in you.

Mother of mercy, have pity on me. I hear all calling you the refuge and hope of sinners. Be, then, my refuge and my hope. For the love of Jesus Christ, your Son, help me.

Give your hand to a poor sinner who commends himself to you and dedicates himself to your lasting service. I praise and thank God who in His mercy has given to me this confidence in you, a sure pledge of my eternal salvation.

It is true that in the past, I, miserable and wretched, have fallen into sin because I did not have recourse to you. But I know that with your help I shall be able to overcome myself. I know, too, that you will help me, if I commend myself to you. But I fear that in the occasions of sin, I may neglect to call upon you and thus run the risk of being lost.

This grace, then, I seek of you; for this I implore you as much as I know and as much as I can:

that in all the attacks of hell I may ever have recourse to you and say to you: "O Mary, help me. O Mother of Perpetual Help, do not let me lose my God."

(3 Hail Marys.)

Mother of Perpetual Help, aid me ever to call upon your powerful name, since your name is the help of the living and the salvation of the dying. Mary most pure, Mary most sweet, grant that your name from this day forth may be to me the very breath of life. Dear Lady, do not delay in coming to help me when I call upon you, for in all the temptations that trouble me, in all the needs of my life, I will ever call upon you, repeating: "Mary, Mary."

What comfort, what sweetness, what confidence, what consolation fills my soul at the sound of your name, at the very thought of you! I give thanks to the Lord, who for my sake has given you a name so sweet, so lovable and so mighty. But I am not content only to speak your name; I will call upon you because I love you. I want that love to remind me always to call you Mother of Perpetual Help.

(3 Hail Marys.)

you are the dispenser of every grace that God grants us in our misery.

For this reason He has made you so powerful, so rich, and so kind that you might help us in our needs.

You are the advocate of the most wretched and abandoned sinners, if they but come to you.

Icon-Our Lady of Perpetual HelpCome to my aid for I commend myself to you.

In your hands I place my eternal salvation; to you I entrust my soul.

Count me among your most faithful servants. Take me under your protection; that is enough for me.

If you protect me, I shall fear nothing: not my sins, because you will obtain for me their pardon and remission; not the evil spirits, because you are mightier than all the powers of Hell; not even Jesus, my Judge, because He is appeased by a single prayer from you.

I fear only that through my own negligence I may forget to recommend myself to you and so lose my soul.

My dear Lady, obtain for me the forgiveness of my sins, love for Jesus, final perseverance, and

the grace to have recourse to you at all times, Mother of Perpetual Help.

(3 Hail Marys.)

St Peregrine

Feast Day: May 1.

O God, who gave to Saint Peregrine an Angel for his companion, the Mother of God for his Teacher, and Jesus as the Physician of his malady, grant we beseech You through his merits that we may on earth intensely love our Holy Angel, the blessed Virgin Mary, and our Savior, and in him bless them forever. Grant that we may receive the favor for which we now petition. We ask this through the same Christ our Lord. Amen.

(Pray 7 Our Fathers, 7 Hail Marys and 7 Glorias with the invocation "Saint Peregrine, pray for us.")

Prayer to Saint Peregrine

Glorious wonder-worker, St. Peregrine, you answered the divine call with a ready spirit, and forsook all the comforts of a life of ease and all the empty honors of the world to dedicate yourself to God in the Order of His holy Mother.

You labored manfully for the salvation of souls. In union with Jesus crucified, you endured painful sufferings with such patience as to deserve to be healed miraculously of an incurable cancer in your leg by a touch of His divine hand.

Obtain for me the grace to answer every call of God and to fulfill His will in all the events of life. Enkindle in my heart a consuming zeal for the salvation of all men.

Deliver me from the infirmities that afflict my body (especially...)

Obtain for me also a perfect resignation to the sufferings it may please God to send me, so that, imitating our crucified Savior and His sorrowful Mother, I may merit eternal glory in heaven.

St. Peregrine, pray for me and for all who invoke your aid.

Prayer to Saint Peregrine

O great St. Peregrine, you have been called 'The Mighty, ' 'The Wonder-Worker, ' because of the numerous miracles which you have obtained from God for those who have had recourse to you.

For so many years you bore in your own flesh this cancerous disease that destroys the very fiber of our being, and who had recourse to the source of all grace when the power of man could do no more. You were favored with the vision of Jesus coming down from His Cross to heal your affliction. Ask of God and Our Lady, the cure of the sick whom we entrust to you.

(Pause here and silently recall the names of the sick for whom you are praying)

Aided in this way by your powerful intercession, we shall sing to God, now and for all eternity, a song of gratitude for His great goodness and mercy.

Amen.

The Memorare

Can be said 9 consecutive times.

Remember, O most gracious Virgin Mary, that never was it known that anyone who fled to thy protection, implored thy help, or sought thine intercession was left unaided.

Inspired by this confidence, I fly unto thee, O Virgin of virgins, my mother; to thee do I come, before thee I stand, sinful and sorrowful. O Mother of the Word Incarnate, despise not my petitions, but in thy mercy hear and answer me.

Amen.

St. Dymphna

Feast Day: May 15.

(Patron Saint for Mental Illness)

Lord, our God, you graciously chose St. Dymphna as patroness of those afflicted with mental and nervous disorders. She is thus an inspiration and a symbol of charity to the thousands who ask her intercession.

Please grant, Lord,

Through the prayers of this pure youthful martyr, relief and consolation to all suffering such trials, and especially those for whom we pray.

(Here you mention those for whom you wish to pray.)

We beg You, Lord, to hear the prayers of St. Dymphna on our behalf. Grant all those for whom we pray patience in their sufferings and resignation to Your divine will. Please fill them with hope, and grant them the relief and cure they so much desire.

We ask this through Christ our Lord

Who suffered agony in the garden.

Amen.

Saint Dymphna, a great wonder worker in every affliction of mind and body, I humbly implore your powerful intercession with Jesus through Mary, the health of the sick.

You are filled with love and compassion for the thousands of patients brought to your shrine for centuries and for those who cannot come to your shrine but invoke you in their homes or in hospitals. Show the same love and compassion toward me, your faithful client. The many miracles you have wrought through your intercession give me great confidence that you will help me in my present need (mentions your request).

I am confident in obtaining my request, if it is for the greater glory of God and the good of my soul. For the sake of Jesus and Mary, whom you loved so earnestly, and for whom you offered your life in martyrdom, grant my prayer.

St Dymphna, young and beautiful, innocent and pure, help me to imitate your love of purity. You chose to be martyred by your own father's sword rather than consent to sin. Give me strength and courage in fighting off the temptations of the world and evil desires.

As you have given all the love of your heart to Jesus, help me to love God with my whole heart and serve Him faithfully. As you bore the persecution of your father and the suffering of an exile so patiently, obtain for me the patience

I need to accept the trials of my life with loving resignation to the Will of God.

Our Lady Of Mount Carmel

Feast Day: July 16.

Oh, most beautiful flower of Mount Carmel, fruitful vine, splendor of Heaven.

Oh, Blessed Mother of the Son of God; Immaculate Virgin, assist me in my necessity.

Oh, Star of the Sea, help me and show me you are my Mother.

Oh, Holy Mary, Mother of God, Queen of Heaven and Earth, I humbly beseech you from the bottom of my heart to succor me in my necessity.

(Mention your request here)

There are none that can withstand your power.

Oh, Mary, conceived without sin, pray for us who have recourse to thee. (say three times).

Holy Mary, I place this prayer in your hands. (say three times).

Amen.

St. Rita of Cascia

(Patroness of impossible causes)

Feast Day: May 24.

O Holy Patroness of those in need, St. Rita, whose pleadings before thy Divine Lord are almost irresistible, who for thy lavishness in granting favors hast been called the Advocate of the Hopeless and even of the impossible. St. Rita, so humble, so pure, so mortified, so patient and of such compassionate love for thy Crucified Jesus, that thou couldst obtain from Him whatsoever thou askest, on account of which all confidently have recourse to thee expecting, if not always relief, at least comfort; be propitious to our petition, showing thy power with God on behalf of thy suppliant; be lavish to us, as thou hast been in so many wonderful cases, for the greater glory of God, for the spreading of thine own devotion, and for the consolation of those who trust in thee.

We promise, if our petition is granted, to glorify thee by making know thy favor, to bless and sing thy praises forever. Relying then upon thy merits and power before the Sacred Heart of Jesus, we pray thee grant that [here mention your request].

By the singular merits of thy childhood,

Obtain for us our request.

By thy perfect union with the Divine Will,

Obtain for us our request.

By thy heroic sufferings during thy married life,

Obtain for us our request.

By the consolation thou didst experience at the conversion of thy husband,

Obtain for us our request.

By the sacrIfice of thy children rather than see them grievously offend God,

Obtain for us our request.

By the miraculous entrance into the convent,

Obtain for us our request.

By thy severe penances and thrice daily bloody scourgings,

Obtain for us our request.

By the suffering caused by the wound thou didst receive from the thorn of thy Crucified Savior,

Obtain for us our request.

By the Divine love which consumed thy heart,

Obtain for us our request.

By that remarkable devotion to the Blessed Sacrament,

Obtain for us our request.

On which alone thou didst exist for four years,

Obtain for us our request.

By the happiness with which thou didst part from thy trials to join thy Divine Spouse,

Obtain for us our request.

By the perfect example thou gavest to people of every state of life.

Obtain for us our request.

Pray for us, O holy St. Rita,

That we may be made worthy of the promises of Christ.

Let us pray:

O God, Who in Thine infinite tenderness hast vouchsafed to regard the prayer of Thy servant, Blessed Rita, and dost grant to her supplication that which is impossible to human foresight, skill and efforts, in reward of her compassionate love and firm reliance on Thy promise, have pity on our adversity and succor us in our calamities, that the unbeliever may know Thou art the recompense of the humble, the defense of the helpless, and the strength of those who trust in Thee, through Jesus Christ, Our Lord.

Amen.

St. Anne

Feast Day: July 26.

Glorious Saint Anne, filled with compassion for those who invoke you and with love; for those who suffer, heavily laden with the weight of their troubles, I cast myself at your feet and humbly beg of you to take the present affair which I recommend to you under your special protection.

(Here ask for the favor you wish to obtain.)

Vouchsafe to recommend it to your daughter, the Blessed Virgin Mary, and lay it before the throne of Jesus Christ, so that He may bring it to a happy issue. Cease not to intercede for me until my request is granted. Above all, obtain for me the grace of one day beholding my God face to face, and with You and Holy Mary and all the saints, praising and blessing Almighty God through all eternity. Amen

Immaculate Heart Of Mary

Feast Day: August 22.

O Most Blessed Mother, heart of love, heart of mercy, ever listening, caring, consoling, hear our prayer. As your children, we implore your intercession with Jesus your Son. Receive with understanding and compassion the petitions we place before you today, especially... (special intention).

We are comforted in knowing your heart is ever open to those who ask for your prayer. We trust to your gentle care and intercession, those whom we love and who are sick or lonely or hurting. Help all of us, Holy Mother, to bear our burdens in this life until we may share eternal life and peace with God forever.

Amen.

Our Lady Of Lourdes

Feast Day: February 11.

Be blessed, O most pure Virgin, for having vouchsafed to manifest your shining with life, sweetness and beauty, in the Grotto of Lourdes, saying to the child, St. Bernadette: 'I am the Immaculate Conception. ' A thousand times we congratulate you upon your Immaculate Conception. And now, O ever Immaculate Virgin, Mother of mercy, Health of the sick, Refuge of sinners, Comforter of the afflicted, you know our wants, our troubles, our sufferings deign to cast upon us a look of mercy.

By appearing in the Grotto of Lourdes, you were pleased to make it a privileged sanctuary, whence you dispense your favors, and already many have obtained the cure of their infirmities, both spiritual and physical. We come, therefore, with the most unbounded confidence to implore your maternal intercession. Obtain for us, O loving Mother, the granting of our request.

(state your request)

Through gratitude for your favors, we will endeavor to imitate your virtues, that we may one day share your glory.

Our Lady of Lourdes, Mother of Christ, you had influence with your divine son while upon earth. You have the same influence now in Heaven. Pray for us; obtain for us from your Divine Son our special requests if it be the Divine Will. Amen.

Our Lady of Lourdes, pray for us.

Saint Bernadette, pray for us.

Amen.

St. Philomena

Feast Day: August 11.

We beseech Thee, O Lord, to grant us the pardon of our sins by the intercession of Saint Philomena, virgin and martyr, who was always pleasing in Thy sight by her eminent chastity and by the profession of every virtue. Amen.

Illustrious virgin and martyr, Saint Philomena, behold me prostrate before the throne whereupon it has pleased the Most Holy Trinity to place thee. Full of confidence in thy protection, I entreat thee to intercede for me with God, from the heights of Heaven deign to cast a glance upon thy humble client! Spouse of Christ, sustain me in suffering, fortify me in temptation, protect me in the dangers surrounding me, obtain for me the graces necessary to me, and in particular

(Here specify your petition).

Above all, assist me at the hour of my death. Saint Philomena, powerful with God, pray for us. Amen.

O God, Most Holy Trinity, we thank Thee for the graces Thou didst bestow upon the Blessed Virgin Mary, and upon Thy handmaid Philomena, through whose intercession we implore Thy Mercy. Amen.

14 Holy Helpers

The Holy Helpers are:

St. Achatius: May 8th — Headaches

St. Barbara: Dec. 4th — Fever — Sudden death

St. Blaise : Feb. 3rd — Ills of the throat

St. Catherine of Alexandria: Nov. 25th — Sudden death

St. Christopher: July 25th — Plagues — Sudden death

St. Cyriacus: Aug. 8th — Temptations

St. Denis: Oct. 9th — Headaches

St. Erasmus (Elmo): June 2nd — Abdominal maladies

St. Eustachius (Eustace): Sep. 20th — Family trouble

St. George: Apr. 23rd — Protection of domestic animals

St. Giles (Aegidius): Sep.1st — Plagues — Good Confession

St. Margaret of Antioch: July 20th — Safe childbirth

St. Pantaleone: July 27th — Physicians

St. Vitus (St. Guy):June 15th — Epilepsy

Prayer

Great princes and princesses of Heaven, Holy Helpers, who sacrificed to God all your earthly possessions, wealth, enjoyments, and even life, and who now are crowned in Heaven in the secure delight of eternal bliss and glory, have compassion on me, a poor sinner in this valley of tears. Obtain for me from God, Who loves you and for Whom you gave up all things, the strength to bear patiently all the trials of this life, to overcome all temptations, and to persevere in God's service to the end. So that, one day, I too may be received into your company, to praise and glorify Him, the supreme Lord, Whose beatific vision you enjoy, and Whom you praise and glorify for ever. Amen.

St Lucy

Feast Day: December 13.

(Patron Saint for eyes)

O St Lucy, you preferred to let your eyes be torn out instead of denying the faith and defiling your soul; and God, through an extraordinary miracle, replaced them with another pair of sound and perfect eyes to reward your virtue and faith, appointing you as the protector against eye diseases. I come to you for you to protect my eyesight and to heal the illness in my eyes.

O St Lucy, preserve the light of my eyes so that I may see the beauties of creation, the glow of the sun, the colour of the flowers and the smile of children.

Preserve also the eyes of my soul, the faith, through which I can know my God, understand His teachings, recognise His love for me and never miss the road that leads me to where you, St Lucy, can be found in the company of the angels and saints.

St Lucy, protect my eyes and preserve my faith. Amen.

(Say: 3 "Our Father", 3 "Hail Mary", 3 "Glory be".)

O! Glorious St Lucy, Virgin and Martyr, you greatly glorified the Lord by preferring to sacrifice your life rather than be unfaithful. Come to our aid and, through the love of this same most loveable Lord, save us from all infirmities of the eyes and the danger of losing them.

Through your powerful intercession, may we spend our life in the peace of the Lord and be able to see Him with our transfigured eyes in the eternal splendour of the Celestial Homeland. Amen.

St Lucy, pray for us and for the most needy, to Christ our Lord. Amen.

St. Apollonia

Feast Day: February 9.

(Patron Saint of teeth and mouth.)

O Glorious Apollonia, patron saint of dentistry and refuge to all those suffering from diseases of the teeth, I consecrate myself to thee, beseeching thee to number me among thy clients. Assist me by your intercession with God in my daily work and intercede with Him to obtain for me a happy death. Pray that my heart like thine may be inflamed with the love of Jesus and Mary, through Christ our Lord. Amen. O My God, bring me safe through temptation and strengthen me as thou didst our own patron Apollonia, through Christ our Lord. Amen

St. Cosmas and Damian

Feast Day: September 26.

O Physicians of souls, Saints Cosmas and Damian, stand before the Lord of All and ask Him to heal me and all those dear to me of any spiritual ills we may endure.

Drive away from us all sin and sadness of mind, all darkness and despair.

Make us then willing and loving servants of Christ, following your holy example of detachment from the things of this world and care for the needs of our neighbors.

On the glorious day of the Universal Resurrection may we shine with you in the full health of our nature restored by the mercies of Jesus who lives and reigns forever and ever.

Amen.

St. Martha

(Feast Day: July 29)

To be said for 9 consecutive Tuesdays.

Light a candle before or after prayer.

Saint Martha, I resort to thy aid and protection. As proof of my affection and faith, I offer thee this light, which I shall burn every Tuesday. Comfort me in all my difficulties and through the great favors thou didst enjoy when the Savior was lodged in thy house, intercede for my family, that we be provided for in our neccessities. I ask of thee, Saint Martha, to overcome all difficulties as thou didst overcome the dragon which thou hadst at thy feet.

In the name of the Father and of the Son and of the Holy Spirit.

Amen.

Recite the following prayers...

Our Father...

Hail Mary...

Glory Be...

St. Andrew Christmas Novena

To be said 15 times a day from November 30 to December 24.

Hail and blessed be the hour and moment in which the Son of God was born of the most pure Virgin Mary, at midnight, in Bethlehem, in piercing cold. In that hour vouchsafe, I beseech Thee, O my God, to hear my prayer and grant my desires through the merits of Our Savior Jesus Christ, and of His blessed Mother.

Amen.